WHITE~KNUCKLE FAITH

Trusting God in Times of Crisis

All praise to God, the Father of our Lord Jesus Christ.
God is our merciful Father and the source of all com-
fort. He comforts us in all our troubles so that we can
comfort others. When they are troubled, we will be able
to give them the same comfort God has given us.
2 Corinthians 1:3-4 Living Bible

By Dave and Jeanne Kaufman

ISBN: 978-1-57579-350-4

Library of Congress Control Number: 2007920146

Rollercoaster cover photo courtesy
of Jason from coasterphotos.com.

First printing, February 2007
Second printing, September 2007

Printed in the United States of America

PINE HILL PRESS
4000 West 57th Street
Sioux Falls, SD 57106

Dedication:

To Jesus Christ, Who has sustained
us in this journey of faith. His love
and power have brought
peace and victory to our family.

To each other as husband and wife. We have
worked together as a "team" to complete this
work and to advance the Kingdom of God.

To our children, as they share
in this victory that Christ has won.

A Special Thanks:

To the many people who have encouraged
us through the years to stand in faith
and to not give up.

To Kathy Spolum for her labors of love
in editing and proofing this book.

To Jennifer Walker for developing the
design for the cover.

Endorsements

From Minnesota~

Pastor Dave and Jeanne Kaufman tell with passion the story of such a tenacious, persistent, and enduring faith, during one of the greatest trials that any family could go through. The Kaufmans share about contending for their little daughter Angela's life for several years, as an unknown enemy, a virulent disease, was attacking and destroying her body. That faith is so deeply anchored in the Person, the character, and the promises of God for healing, through His Living Word, His Son, Jesus Christ! Every person who is struggling personally, or has a loved one with chronic, debilitating, or acute disease, should read this heart-lifting, encouraging story of real life faith in action. The Kaufmans are ordinary people, with an extraordinary trust in an amazing God. Their story will build your faith to believe for what is impossible, to find a way where there seems to be no way, and to trust fully in Jesus Christ. We have watched as their infectious and positive faith has permeated their entire congregation, their city, the medical community and every person and place the Lord calls them to share this wonderful story of His great love and His power to heal!

Pastors Jim & Ramona Rickard
Brooklyn Park, Minnesota
Founders of:
RAIN – Resurrection Apostolic International Network
The International Association of Healing Ministries
Midwest Apostolic Prophetic Conference

From Colorado-

Dave and Jeanne Kaufman have been our dear friends since college days. We held Angela and Ryan soon after they were born. We were on vacation together in the Black Hills when Angela first became ill. We joined numbers of people who fasted and prayed for Angela with seemingly no results. As the Kaufmans steadfastly clung to the Word of God, year after year, and praised their way to overcoming faith, we marveled. Normally, the more intimately one knows people, the less one is able to acknowledge true greatness. Having watched this saga from the beginning to the end, there is no family in our lives that we love and admire more than the Kaufmans. They are evidence that the purest gold is produced by the most intense refining. The faith principles in this book are not pleasant platitudes, but rather, the bread of life from which they partook daily to sustain themselves. Dave and Jeanne are practitioners, not theorists. They responded to the grace that our Father God, imparted to them with an indomitable, courageous and overcoming faith. May you be as inspired as you read this book as we have been watching their lives for the past 35 years. Prepare to be astonished and blessed!

Paul and Peggy Parker
Mountain Plains Regional Superintendent
Open Bible Churches
Colorado Springs, Colorado

From South Dakota~

Evelyn and I have had the privilege of knowing the Kaufmans for 25 years. We have stayed in each other's homes and co-labored in the ministry together. They are solid and unwavering in their faith and in their walk with God. No doubt you've heard the saying, "everything that glitters is not gold," but let me tell you, these two are the "real deal!" They fought, unwavering, for their daughter's healing. When others would have quit in the fight, they persevered and won! In Oral Roberts' great healing campaigns they used to sing the song, "God is a good God, every heartache He understands... what He's done for others, He will do for you." I believe this fantastic testimony will inspire you to be increased in your own faith. Please enjoy!

Gary D. Johnson, Sr. Pastor
Dove Christian Center
Rapid City, South Dakota

From South Dakota-

Little did Pastor Dave and Jeanne Kaufman know when they left Faith Temple Church on their wedding day in 1975 that they would be so challenged in their ministry, their family and their faith! These servants, in the strength of the Lord, rose to the task of standing against adversity. They have seen victory and continue to walk with overcoming faith. Enjoy this amazing book!

Pastor Jeff Hayes
Faith Temple Church
Sioux Falls, South Dakota

From Kansas-

Dave and Jeanne Kaufman are living examples of not only persevering faith, but of constantly reaching out in all directions with compassion and love. Reading this book will be listening to one of the 21st century fathers. They are a rare couple who manifest the gift of hospitality in very unique ways.

Pastor Ernie and Dee Gruen
Grace & Mercy Ministries
Lenexa, Kansas

From Minnesota-

White-Knuckle Faith is a fabulous book that will stir your faith in many areas of your life. It will also bring great hope to those facing physical trials. This book is a great blend of story, instruction and promise through scripture, an exhortation to lift your hopes in God. God bless the Kaufman family for sharing their story to encourage others!

Pastor Tim Burt
Living Word Christian Center
Brooklyn Park, Minnesota

Introduction

RIDING THE ROLLER COASTER

When you are tempted to give up, don't quit! When you are discouraged and frustrated, keep praying! When you feel tired and oppressed, put on that garment of praise! When you feel lonely and that nobody cares, get up and go to church! You must be willing and determined to hold on to the promises of God for as long as it takes. That could be one hour, one day, or twelve years. You must just hold on with "WHITE-KNUCKLE FAITH."

When I was riding a roller coaster, I looked down at my hands holding the lap bar. I was holding on so tight that my knuckles were white. So it is with God. If you are facing adversity, this is not the time to walk away from God but to hold on to Him. This is the time to run into His loving arms.

This book will inspire your faith and enable you to stand victoriously in the midst of adversity. It will help you through the roller coaster of emotions that can accompany long-term illness. You can have a steady walk of faith and receive the promises of God's Word that are available for you today.

Table of Contents

Life Can Change in a Moment

The room was cool. Nurses were checking on the patients to monitor their conditions. Angela, our six-year old daughter, had just had a biopsy on her deltoid muscle, and she was still asleep in the recovery room at Sioux Valley Hospital in Sioux Falls, South Dakota in August 1983. She weighed just fifty-three pounds. I sat staring off into space thinking how quickly our lives had changed. Only three months before, we were the picture-perfect, all-American family. Two children, a girl and a boy. A wonderful marriage. Living in our own home. I was the pastor of a two-year old church. Everything had gone so well for us.

We met each other while we were still in college at South Dakota State University in Brookings, South Dakota. We both had previously become Christians. We met in a restaurant just before I graduated. Both of us were excited about serving God. Jeanne had already taken some missions trips to the Soviet Union, Switzerland, Ireland and Mexico. Nothing stood in her way of following the Lord with all of her heart. Jeanne has a bold and confident faith for God to do miracles.

While we were dating, Dave's interest in God's plan for his life grew. Shortly, after we were engaged to be married, Dave, too, was off on a missions trip to the Far East. He was gone for six weeks ministering in the Philippine Islands and Hong Kong. God was opening doors everywhere, and we purposed to walk through each one. The opportunities came to sing and proclaim the Gospel in churches, schools, businesses and on Philippine television. Even government institutions were opened to us. Our faith soared like an eagle. The power of the Holy Spirit rested upon us.

We were married in November 1975, at Faith Temple Church in Sioux Falls, South Dakota. We lived in Sioux Falls for a few years. Jeanne worked briefly before our first child was born. Dave worked in the business field even though that wasn't his college major. Having been a college athlete, he traveled for the Fellowship of Christian Athletes and took the opportunities to speak at Bible studies, schools and church banquets.

We rented a quaint little house in Sioux Falls where we attended church regularly and had many friends. Our lives were so blessed. Angela was born in February 1977. We were thrilled to be parents. Angela was in great health and was one of those children that you just never have a problem with. Our son, Ryan, was born in May 1978. We had the perfect family with a boy and a girl. Ryan was also a great baby with a wonderful temperament.

The summer after Ryan was born, we decided to move fifty miles north near Brookings, South Dakota. Dave had the opportunity to study for his ministerial degree while continuing to work. He later worked as the director of a local Teen Challenge program for a couple of years before entering the pastoral ministry full time. We pioneered our nondenominational church ministry in the spring of 1981.

Our children were healthy, fun-loving, athletic kids. Angela entered kindergarten in September 1982. Everything about our children's health had been normal until the spring of 1983. After an afternoon of fishing at an area lake, both children came down with a rash on their hands. It all seemed rather innocuous at the time. We thought it was nothing to be overly concerned about. After a few days, the rash on Ryan's hands disappeared but the rash on Angela's seemed to get worse.

Over the summer, we watched Angela's condition deteriorate before our eyes. The doctors at the local clinic were baffled by her symptoms. Soon, we could see that she seemed to be getting weak in her body. She was unable to do the normal activities like running, jumping and playing that a healthy six-year old could do. The progressive muscle weakness came on suddenly. The local doctor recommended that we get advice from a specialist in Sioux Falls.

It's amazing how the circumstances of life can change so fast. The doctors suspected that Angela had somehow contracted a rare disease that was fiercely attacking her immune system. We were at a point where we were helping Angela to get out of bed in the morning. She could no longer go up or down stairs without assistance. The doctors at Central Plains Clinic in Sioux Falls began basic tests on Angela but at our urging they expedited their procedures. Every day, Angela's condition worsened, and we had no time to waste. We realized we were up against a fierce enemy. People all around us were praying with us for Angela. We were convinced that this would pass, and it would all just be like a bad dream. That didn't happen.

The more tests the doctors ran at Central Plains, the more sober they became. They began to rule out anything that was ordinary and easy to treat. Soon they suggested to us their worst fears. They thought Angela might possibly have a rare muscle and skin disease called "Dermatomyositis." How strange it was to hear those words spoken to us. Surely this would not be the case. We were praying, faith-filled Christians who were believing the Word of God. How could our daughter be so sick?

The doctors said they needed to perform a muscle biopsy to get a conclusive diagnosis of her disease. We agreed. The biopsy is normally a routine procedure with few risks, but that was not to be the case with Angela. The surgery went well, but in the recovery room Angela's body went into shock. She was shaking badly on the bed, but the medical staff thought that she was just cold from the room temperature. Finally at our urging, the medical staff realized that her condition was serious.

Her body had gone into shock. The attending nurses and medical personnel did not notice that her temperature had spiked to 104. The IV had already been removed, so a doctor rushed in to help get another one started. Her veins were collapsing, and her condition worsened before our eyes. Now one doctor and three nurses feverishly worked on Angela to no avail. They were losing her. They punctured both arms and ankles trying to get an IV in, but they couldn't. A thousand thoughts run through your mind. "Your daughter is dying." "Where is God?" "Why aren't our prayers being answered?" All I could feel was this heavy cloud of death hanging over us.

God can move in any situation if we give Him the opportunity. Nothing is too difficult for Him. What man cannot do, God is well able to perform. In these horrible circumstances, the voice of the Lord calmly came to me and said, "Why don't you praise Me?" I was surprised by the words. "Why don't I praise You?" I thought, " What should I praise You for? My daughter is dying before my eyes and You haven't done anything." And the Lord spoke again and simply said, " I am not your problem, I am your ANSWER."

I felt nothing emotionally. I felt no anointing. The circumstances were screaming in my ears to panic. But I stepped back from the bed and the medical team who was trying to save our daughter, and I pulled the curtain that was by the bed. Jeanne was by the bed praying out loud with Angela and the nurse said, "Keep praying." Out of sheer obedience to what the voice of the Lord had spoken, I lifted my hands and began to worship God. At that moment, I learned what it meant to bring a "sacrifice of praise" to the Lord.

Anyone can praise God when everything is going his or her way, but what about in the tough times when you face difficult circumstances? Hebrews 13:15 says, "By Him therefore, let us offer the sacrifice of praise to God continually, that is, the fruit of our lips giving thanks unto His name."

As I began to sing praises to God, something broke in me. Many people blame God for all of their problems without recognizing that our real adversary is the devil. 1 Peter 5:8 tells us, " Be sober, be vigilant; because your adversary the devil, as a roaring lion, is walking about, seeking whom he may devour." I realized that God is on our side. He loves me and our daughter. HE IS MY ANSWER!

I sang out loud in the Spirit. I praised Him because He is good and His mercy endures forever. It was totally amazing . The more I sang, the more the presence of the Lord came in our midst. I didn't care who heard me; my pride and the fear of what others may think of me was gone. After several minutes, the most wonderful PEACE fell on us.

Angela's condition changed before our eyes. The nurse counted down the degrees as her temperature dropped. Her body stopped shaking. They never were able to get an IV in, but her condition stabilized in an instant. The doctor leaned back from her bed with beads of sweat on his forehead and a sigh of relief. Everyone was quiet and no one could mistake the wonderful presence of God that had flooded the room. Angela spent a couple of days in the hospital as they tried to determine what medications to give her to fight the disease.

This picture of Angela and her brother, Ryan, was taken in September 1983, shortly after she had her muscle biopsy. We put pillows behind her for comfort and support.

Prayer:
Lord, I believe that You are greater than anything that I face today. I choose to praise You and to put my faith and trust in Jesus Christ. I receive Your peace right now. Thank you for helping me in my time of need. In the name of Jesus. Amen.

Hearing a Bad Report

B ad reports come to people every day all over the world. You are not alone when you might receive bad news. Accidents, doctors' reports, a bad diagnosis, or a phone call in the night can all bring a shock to our lives. We live in a fallen world, therefore, we should not be surprised if some day, we find ourselves facing our own bad report. It could be as simple as hearing we did not get the pay raise or promotion that we had hoped for, or hearing that your child did not get a part in the school play. How we face the bad reports that have small consequences, will lay a foundation for bigger things.

In the book of Numbers , Chapter 13, Moses was directed by God to send spies into the promised land and to bring back a report. Now, the Lord had already told the Israelites that He had given them the land and that they were to possess it. The issue was never "IF" they should go into the land. So Moses chose one leader out of each tribe of Israel to form a team of twelve men. These men were "leaders" and not novices. They were supposed to be the spiritually mature ones. They went with the directions that Moses gave to them and stayed in the Land of Promise for forty days. When they returned they began to give a glowing report of all the wealth and prosperity that they saw in the land.

Then they included the facts that the people were strong and the cities were fortified and that there were many obstacles to face. All of this was indeed true, but the more that they talked about the problems and the obstacles, the more discouraged they became. They soon saw themselves as "grasshoppers" (verse 33) in comparison to their enemies. If you have a "grasshopper mentality" you will never overcome your adversary. You must see yourself as God sees you. In Christ, you are more than a conqueror (Romans 8:37)! Greater is He that is in you than he that is in the world (1 John 4:4).

The twelve spies already were told that God had given them the land, but ten of them decided that they were not able to possess or conquer the land. In their eyes, it seemed like a suicide mission. Therefore the Bible says that they brought an evil report to the children of Israel. They caused the people to mourn. If God has spoken His will, you can be assured that He will stand behind His Word to perform it. Now, two of the spies were named Joshua and Caleb. These two men quieted the people enough to say that indeed there were obstacles, but they were still well able to go up and to possess the land. Even though they reminded the people of what God had spoken, the people drew the wrong conclusion that they should not go into the land.

You will be faced with a bad report many times in your life. The circumstances will be a "report" to your mind and to your emotions, but you must weigh that report with the "report" that you receive from the Word of God. Who do you suppose has more authority? The doctor, the banker, the teacher, the employer, or God Himself? We are going to choose the Word of God over all of our other circumstances. We are not denying that our circumstances exist, but we are expressing our faith in God that He is greater than all that we face. You do not have to be intimidated into accepting the evil report. Just keep your eyes on Jesus and His promises and allow His wonderful peace to rule in your heart.

A team of physicians was assembled due to the complexity of Angela's case. Dr. Walter Drymalski, a rheumatologist at Central Plains Clinic, became the lead physician for us. He usually did not treat children, but this was not an ordinary situation.

His medical competence was complemented by his caring kindness toward us. He was extremely helpful to us over twelve years of therapy.

Dermatomyositis is an autoimmune disease that inflames the skin and the muscles. When the immune system mistakes self tissue for nonself and mounts an inappropriate attack, the result is an autoimmune disease. Some of Angela's T cells were attacking her own body. The Muscular Dystrophy Association has researched this disease for years for a cause and a cure. Much of our body is muscle tissue, including our internal organs. So at worse, dermatomyositis can severely affect your lungs, heart, kidneys and liver.

The treatments for this disease involved immuno-suppressant medications to help decrease the cells that were fighting Angela's own body. In Angela's situation, her face, arms, legs, back, heart, lungs, liver and kidneys were all affected by dermatomyositis. High doses of prednisone were initially used, but later the drugs of methotrexate and plaquenil were added to try to control the disease.

Prednisone is in a class of drugs called steroids. It reduces swelling and inflammation, and decreases the body's ability to fight infections. Some side effects include: nausea, fatigue, weight gain, muscle weakness, thinning of the skin, increased facial hair and a suppressed immune system.

Methotrexate is classified as an antimetabolite drug, which means it is capable of blocking the metabolism of cells. As a result of this effect, it has been found helpful in treating certain diseases associated with abnormally rapid cell growth. For Angela, it seemed to help, in part by altering aspects of the immune function which may play a role in causing a rheumatic disease like dermatomyositis. It has severe side effects that include: nausea, decreased appetite, hair loss, dizziness, drowsiness, liver and kidney problems and a suppressed immune system.

Plaquenil was originally developed to fight the malaria infection. Later it was also discovered to decrease the muscle inflammation associated with diseases like dermatomyositis. The risks involve stomach nausea and vision problems in the eyes.

All of these drugs were very difficult for us to accept. Our family had always experienced good health to this point. It had been rare for us to even take an aspirin. Now our daughter needed strong medications with harsh side effects just to live. When Angela would take pills or receive IV treatments, we always prayed that God would enhance the good effects in the medication and eliminate the bad.

At one point, we noticed that it became increasingly difficult for Angela to sing in church or to clap her hands. Doctors confirmed that much of her body was adversely affected. At times she only spoke with puffing breaths as she tried to get air into her lungs. A pulmonary breathing test revealed that she had lost 50% of her breathing capacity. The peristalsis (lack of muscle movement) in her throat was hindered to the point that her ability to swallow food or liquids was extremely difficult. We ground her food and hand fed her so that she wouldn't choke. Even when she would drink milk, her muscle reflex would cause some of it to come out of her nose.

Of course, we wanted to care for her teeth too, but she was unable to spit the toothpaste out, so we would pull it out again with an eyedropper. Her leg muscle strength was diminished so we had to carry her up or down steps and lift her into the car. For a period of time, she was unable to turn over in bed, so we would periodically get up each night to turn her so that she could sleep in different positions.

After 24 months of battling this affliction, it seemed like the doctor's office was a second home. Blood tests were too numerous to count any more.

It was hard to remember what it was like to have a home without any sickness. In 1985, the rheumatologist recommended that we try the "Bolus Therapy." This involved three days of IV treatments using solu-medrol. It was repeated every month for four months. The doctors had hoped that this would stabilize the disease but wrote in her records, "Patient has not responded significantly to the steroid boluses."At times we felt spiritually numb from all of the negative reports, but we would hold on to God's Word by singing and confessing His wonderful promises. Then we heard of another doctor who was a specialist researching this disease. We thought this person might have some specific insight into Angela's situation.

In October of 1985, we made arrangements and traveled to the University of Kansas Medical Center in Kansas City. We met Dr. Carol Lindsley, a Pediatric Rheumatologist, who was seeing children with dermatomyositis. At that time, she was the nation's foremost authority for this disease. Angela had now been sick for more than two years, and we hoped for some sort of breakthrough.

We arrived early at the hospital on a cold and rainy morning. The doctor spent an entire day with us running many tests and assuring us that they were doing everything that they could. By 5:00 in the afternoon, a special meeting was arranged. We were escorted into a private room with a conference table to meet with the specialist and another staff member to witness what was said to us. Angela was resting in another room. It was one of those meetings that you wish you could avoid. We prepared our hearts for the report that was coming.

Dr. Lindsley is an absolutely wonderful doctor with great people skills. Dermatomyositis is extremely rare in children, but this doctor had examined dozens of cases from around the country. She calmly explained to us that Angela was in the worse 10% of cases that they had ever seen. Then she informed us that Angela had "cardiac enlargement and signs of congestive heart failure." Her heart was twice the size of normal due to inflammation, and the doctor quietly said that she could die at any time from this condition. Inflammation of the heart muscle is extremely dangerous. This is a report that would be more common for an elderly person. Angela was only eight-years old.

We sat there in silence. The room was quiet. We didn't cry. We didn't panic. The doctor proceeded to explain again her diagnosis of Angela's condition. I asked her if any other new treatments existed that could help Angela. She said, "No." Angela was already receiving the proper medications to treat this problem, but they weren't working. The doctor then asked us, "Do you understand what I just told you?" They had just given us a grave report, and I'm sure they were expecting an emotional scene, but I looked at her and quietly said, "Yes, we do."

This was the second time that we were facing death with Angela. Then I spoke to them and said that maybe there was something they did not understand about us. I thanked them for their medical help but I said that our trust was ultimately in Jesus Christ as our Healer, and He would take care of Angela. They looked amazed at my response but agreed that it would take a higher power to help.

We always looked for opportunities to receive prayer from God's leaders and people. We were staying in a Kansas City motel and Jeanne stayed with Angela as she rested in bed. It was a Wednesday night, so I went to a local church that we were familiar with. They loved us and prayed earnestly for us that night. On the drive home the next day, we had to push out the words "congestive heart failure" from our minds over and over again. We were in a spiritual battle, and we had to replace the bad report in our minds with a good report from the Word of God. We confessed God's healing power and His will to heal Angela. We sang praises in the car and tried to keep our minds on God's faithfulness.

One week later, we had a follow-up visit to the clinic in Sioux Falls where they were to re-examine Angela's enlarged heart. The doctor's report dated October 14, 1985, reads, "A chest X-ray is repeated today and compared with the one done last week (in Kansas City); this now shows a normal cardiac size with definite improvement from the enlargement noted on the last X-ray." Hallelujah! God is still performing miracles and healing the sick today.

Prayer:
God, I choose to believe Your Word above my circumstances. I lift my eyes away from my problems, and I thank You for Your promises in the Bible. I choose to rest in You today. In the name of Jesus. Amen.

Facing the Lies

Anyone who faces a long-term illness, will face circumstances that will try to destroy his or her faith in God. You pray hard, but you might see very little results. You read your Bible and confess the Word, but it might seem like nothing ever changes. Then you might have people who seem like "Job's friends." They have all kinds of suggestions of what you should do, but they themselves have a hard time having victory over the common cold. Some people would simply suggest that Angela's disease was the will of God. Some thought that God was trying to teach us something. Others mentioned that everything that happens is God's purpose, so we should just accept the sickness. All of these comments were subtle distractions that kept trying to erode our faith. Here is a good question, "What does the Bible say about healing?"

In the midst of a battle, it is of the utmost importance to know who is your enemy. 1 Peter 5:8 says, "Be sober, be vigilant; because your ADVERSARY the devil, walks about, seeking whom he may devour." We have an opponent who is trying to do everything that he can to harm us. Acts 10:38 says, "God anointed Jesus of Nazareth with the Holy Spirit and with power: who went about DOING GOOD and healing all that were oppressed of the devil."

In many of the churches today, you will never hear the devil mentioned. Yet the Bible will clearly refer to him as an enemy that Jesus Christ dealt with. Martin Luther definitely understood this principal of spiritual battle when he wrote the great hymn, *A Mighty Fortress Is Our God.*" Just look at Luther's words:

> Vs 1: A mighty fortress is our God,
> A bulwark never failing;
> Our helper He amid the flood
> Of mortal ills prevailing.
> For still our ancient foe,
> Doth seek to work us woe
> His craft and power are great,
> And armed with cruel hate,
> On earth is not his equal.
> Vs 3: And tho this world, with devils filled,
> Should threaten to undo us,
> We will not fear, for God hath willed
> His truth to triumph thru us.

The prince of darkness grim,
    We tremble not for him
His rage we can endure,
    For lo, his doom is sure:
One little word shall fell him.

As we faced a long term illness, we had to keep our theology simple: "GOD IS GOOD, and the devil is bad." As you look in your Bible, you'll observe Jesus was always doing good works. Loving, teaching, healing, touching and blessing were common daily acts of His goodness. In John 10:10, Jesus says that, "The thief [devil] comes to steal, and to kill, and to destroy: I am come that they might have life, and that they might have it more abundantly."

We were experiencing the footprints of the devil. He was stealing our finances with staggering medical bills. He was killing our daughter's life with disease. He was destroying anything that seemed to be a normal family life. Even Ryan, our son, missed out on many fun outdoor activities, because Angela could not spend time outside in the sun. We did not go camping or attend many picnics because the sun would damage her skin and inflame the disease. It's imperative to recognize the enemy's evil attacks so that we can resist them with faith. God is on our side! He is for us! Jesus gave His life so that we can have His abundant life. His life does not include sickness, disease, or tragedy for us.

I have met pastors who believe that if you are not healed after you pray, they assume it is God's will for you to be sick. They would back up their assertion by telling me of fine Christian people, whom they personally knew, who prayed earnestly for healing but weren't healed, and some even died. Their conclusion was that this was God's plan for them.

The problem with this theology is that sincere people put more faith in past "experiences" than in the Word of God. We cannot think that our faith is so perfect that all of our experiences line up with God's will. THE WORD OF GOD IS THE WILL OF GOD. Do your experiences line up with what Jesus did in the Bible? Jesus always healed people. He never gave them a sickness.

Now I have to stop and think, how would I like to serve a God who is planning good things for some and awful things for others? Jeremiah 29:11 says that His plans for us are for good and not for evil, so that you might know what to expect in the future. I'm so glad that God is not planning a bad day for you. He doesn't have a nice tragedy waiting for you around the corner. He is not anticipating the day that He can give you that bad diagnosis. No! God is a good God who loves you with an everlasting love. James 1:17 says that there is no shadow of turning in Him. He will not turn on you tomorrow. He will always be by your side when you call on His Name.

Some people say that God is bringing the storms of life on you so that He can teach you something. Funny thing is, they never seem to know "what it is" He is teaching them. God is accused of doing so many bad things today that if He, as our Father, was brought into a Social Services agency, they would lock Him up in prison for being a sadistic parent. Jesus said in John 15:3 that you are pruned through the Word which I have spoken to you. This verse shows that we are not pruned by hard experiences, but by the Word of God.

I have seen many people who were bitter against God because someone taught them that God had caused their bad situation to teach them something. That is not good news. JESUS WENT ABOUT DOING GOOD (Acts 10:38)! Matthew 4:23 says that Jesus went about all the countryside healing all manner of sickness and all manner of disease among the people. So what did the people do? Verse 24 says that "they brought unto Him all that were sick with various diseases and those oppressed by the devil, and HE HEALED THEM." It was easy for the people to come to Jesus because they knew He was doing GOOD things.

The goodness of God makes you want to run into the arms of Jesus Christ. 2 Corinthians 1:20 says, "For all the promises of God in Him are yes, and in Him amen, unto the glory of God by us." God does not favor some people more than others. He has made all of His good promises for an abundant life available to every one of us. We must raise our level of faith and claim what we need today. Isaiah 53: 4 says that "surely He has carried our diseases and carried our pain." If He already did that for us, then we don't have to do it. Verse 5 says that "He was wounded for our rebellion and He was bruised for our sins. The chastisement of our peace, health, and prosperity was upon Him, and with His stripes, we are healed." Praise the Lord! Jesus has already won the victory. 1 Peter 2:24 says that "by His stripes you were healed." That is a statement of historical fact. Jesus paid for your healing at the Cross of Calvary. He bowed His head on the cross and said, "It is finished" (John 19:30). He had fulfilled the prophetic Word in Isaiah 53.

The fact that HEALING IS THE WILL OF GOD was totally ingrained in our hearts. In one particular incident when Angela was critically ill, we laid her on our couch at home and lifted our hearts in prayer and cried. We said, "Lord, we know that healing is Your will and You provided that for us. We don't understand why Angela is not well, but Lord, even if she dies, we will continue to pray for the sick and watch them get healed." This was an extremely difficult prayer. Our hearts were broken for our daughter. We were determined not to base our beliefs on our circumstances but solely on the Word of God. One irony that we experienced was seeing others get healed through prayer but seeing no results in Angela's body.

We continued to resist the lies of the enemy and believe in the goodness of God and His promises for physical healing. We chose to focus on His report above any other reports that people had given us. In spite of our circumstances, we did not miss Sunday worship services. Now, of course you can say that Dave had to be there because he was the pastor, but we realized that we must come to worship so that we could allow His presence and the encouragement of other Christians to refresh us.

We would make the effort with a critically ill child to get up early in the morning. It took extra time to help Angela to eat, to get dressed and to bandage the calcinosis sores on her arms. Then we would help her to the car. You might think that because we were going to church that everything would be so peaceful, and we would always have smiles on our faces. Normal, healthy families fight spiritual battles getting up to go to church, let alone our situation. Anyone with young children knows exactly what I am talking about. Everybody faces attacks from the enemy, especially when you are following the Lord.

When we attended church, everyone could see what we were facing. In our church setting, the pastor and his family usually sit on the front row, so it was pretty clear that our daughter was in great need. Even when she was in her worst condition, we would prop her up in a chair with pillows and help her to be as comfortable as possible. It was amazing how the Lord's presence always showed up to encourage us. Sometimes we would be singing with tears running down our faces. We would hang on every Word from the Bible that would minister to our spirit. Psalm 37:39-40 says, "The salvation of the righteous is of the Lord: He is their strength in time of trouble. And the Lord shall help them, and deliver them: He shall deliver them from the wicked, and save them, because they trust in Him."

In 1986, Angela got sick with the chicken pox (varicella). This is a childhood sickness that normally has few dangerous effects, but nothing was ordinary for us. Angela's immune system was severely suppressed from the prednisone and methotrexate medications, so her internal organs were exposed to the dangerous effects of this virus. She was put into an isolation room on the pediatric ward of Sioux Valley Hospital. She had two days of IV treatments using acyclovir. After this, she continued to attend school, so we regularly prayed for her impaired immune system to be strengthened and to fight off normal sicknesses.

When you don't have many options in a time of crisis, don't throw away your confidence in the Lord. Hebrews 10:35 says that there is a great promise of reward if we just hold on to Jesus. Don't turn your back on the very One and probably the only One who can help you. Some people stay home from church or isolate themselves from others, but this is your time to be refreshed in the house of God. Make the effort to get around positive people who can encourage and support you in your time of need.

There are many stresses that pull on a marriage. A child with poor health and a lack of finances are just two of them. We found it important to work together as a husband and wife team. You can't look back and change history and it is usually not profitable to second guess your decisions. You must endeavor to find unity together. In spite of what we faced, we never considered divorce. Choose to work together and help each other. Pray together. Talk openly about the problems that you face. Encourage each other on a daily basis. Recognize your human weaknesses and shortcomings. Accept the love and forgiveness that come from Jesus Christ. Keep your focus on Jesus and His Words, and He will help make the rough spots smooth.

The storms of life will come against everyone in varying degrees. Your spiritual foundation will be tested, but with Jesus Christ as your Chief Cornerstone, you do not have to be shaken. In Christ, you can be strong and full of peace even in the midst of a storm. Take the time now to dig deep into the Word of God. Jesus said in John 8:32, "You shall know the truth and the truth shall make you free." The level that you understand the Word of God will be the level of your freedom in your life. Good Bible knowledge can give you confidence in your fight of faith against a cunning enemy.

Cultivate your prayer life. Don't use God like a 911 number, calling only when you need Him.

You can hear His voice and walk closely with Him throughout your day. Put on a garment of praise and worship the Lord. I'm not talking about a church service. I'm talking about a song in your heart to the Lord. When you face a long-term illness, you will face many battles in your mind, but as you sing, your praise will shut the devil's mouth and you won't hear his discouraging words. You will have peace in your mind when you magnify the Lord and think on His goodness.

You can dwell on the positive promises of the Word and focus on the blessings of God that you already are experiencing. The old hymn, "*Count Your Blessings*," is very true. Choose to give a positive report of what the Lord is doing. As bad as our situation was, we could always find people who were worse off than we were. We were holding on to the "Prince of Peace" and keeping our eyes fixed on the "Author and Finisher" of our faith. Psalm 119:165 says, "Great peace have those who love Thy Word."

Prayer:
Father, in the mighty name of Jesus, I resist the adversary, the devil. Thank you for Your truth that is setting me free. Lord, I choose to keep my eyes on You and give You praise. In the name of Jesus. Amen.

Holding on to Hope

Hebrews 11:1 says, " Now faith is the substance of things hoped for, the evidence of things not seen." It is a good thing that we do not walk our spiritual life by our feelings. After we have lived with a long-term illness situation for months and years, we will probably not always feel full of faith. It is so important to realize that we must never give up our hope in God. Hope has power. Hope will help to sustain us in those dark moments. Hope helps us to get up in the morning. Hope believes that better days are ahead. Hope confronts the doctors' reports and believes for a miracle cure. Someone once said, "Being defeated is only a temporary condition, but giving up is what makes it permanent."

Hope can change our circumstances overnight. God causes our hope in Him to grow through the promises in the Bible. Romans 8:24 says, "For we are saved by hope: but hope that is seen is not hope." We must believe that those individual promises are true for our needs. The reality of the Word of God is greater than the physical reality of our circumstances. We hope for the things of God that are not seen with our natural eyesight. True hope has a POSITIVE EXPECTATION. It is the expectation that something good will happen. Even though it was difficult, we tried to see Angela totally healed and living a normal life. Hope will keep you going when you feel like giving up.

God really does care about our healing and health. He gave His life for us and He desires for us to be whole, body, soul, and spirit. As hope grows, it takes on the "substance" of faith. Now we come to believe that God's healing promises are for us specifically. You know that God does hear your prayers. Hebrews 11:2 says that with this faith, we can "obtain a good report." In spite of our circumstances, God is still working in powerful ways on our behalf for His glory.

All of the men and women of the Bible faced huge odds against their success, but with faith in their hearts, they overcame their enemies. They had a good report BEFORE they saw an actual change for the better in their physical circumstances. By faith, we obtained a good report even though we weren't seeing the answer. Negative thoughts and speech are killers of faith. Every day, we would be faced with fears: "What if Angela dies? Where would we hold the funeral? What if we go bankrupt?"

An acronym for FEAR is "False Evidence Appearing Real." Don't speak about everything that you see with your eyes or hear with your ears. The Word of God is more real than your natural circumstances. We had to plant the positive seeds of the God's promises in our minds. Push out that old negative thinking with a fresh scripture. Then actually speak it out loud into the air. There is something powerful in the spoken Word. It splits darkness and brings peace to your mind and body.

Shortly after Angela's diagnosis, we were already facing staggering medical bills. Someone informed us that the Muscular Dystrophy Association, a.k.a. MDA, was researching the disease, Dermatomyositis, and suggested that we visit with them. There are some in Christian circles who think that if you go to a doctor, you are not putting your trust in God. This is far from true. God has blessed us with much wisdom in the medical field and in many areas of life. Doctors have sworn to the Hippocratic Oath and they want you to be well as much as you do. So in our situation, we were open to any help that we could receive from medical science.

Walking into the MDA office, we felt like we were in a different world. People normally talk about the cosmetic aspects of life. "How's the weather? Do you like your job?" The outside world around us seemed so artificial. People were carrying on with their lives, and ours was standing still. We had become keenly aware of the simple issues of life and death. As we came into the office, it was hard to verbalize our daughter's experience. We were telling a story that we wished was only a dream. They listened with great compassion, and said that they were indeed researching this disease and that they would pay for all of our medical bills covering the initial diagnosis.

You see, we were fighting two simultaneous battles on different fronts. The one, of course, was for Angela's healing, while the other was for the finances to pay the bills. We did not have medical insurance at that time. Pioneering a new church ministry had left no extra money for health insurance. Nobody ever plans to get sick. You always hope and assume that you will have good health.

Through the years, Angela would also see a neurologist that the Muscular Dystrophy Association provided to follow her case and learn from her medical tests. This allowed us to stay abreast of any new experimental treatments that would hold any promise for Angela's case. Of course, most people are familiar with the Muscular Dystrophy Association's annual Labor Day weekend MDA Telethon hosted by Jerry Lewis. I remember watching the Jerry Lewis movies as I was growing up and enjoying his humor. The Bible says that "a merry heart does good like a medicine" (Proverbs 17:22). It is good therapy to laugh often.

Many times people turn on the TV during the Labor Day weekend and watch the telethon for a moment and then turn the channel. They probably don't know anyone with a rare disease, and they don't want to think about medical tragedies on a holiday weekend. While some people's lives carry on with little inconvenience, others are living in a different world of hardship. On several Labor Days, we, along with our children, Angela and Ryan, found ourselves sitting on the MDA platform at the KSFY Television studio in Sioux Falls, South Dakota. People gave their vacation day to sit at a phone and take calls for financial pledges for research and to help provide equipment to patients. We were a recipient of some of that financial support. We became well known in the MDA community and the medical community. Medical offices and labs almost seemed as familiar as our own home. Doctors, nurses and support staff all knew us on a first-name basis. We knew that they were doing all that they could to help our daughter to be well again. We thought that with God's help and their help, "How can we fail?"

Someone once said, "If you are given a lemon, make lemonade out of it." The Muscular Dystrophy Association approached us and asked if we would let Angela be the South Dakota State Poster Child for MDA. This wasn't exactly the type of honor that we were looking for. Any parent loves it when their child is recognized for his or her achievements but this, of course, was a little different. By accepting this position, we knew that not only would we represent the Muscular Dystrophy Association across our state at various functions, but more importantly, we had the opportunity to give HOPE to others who were suffering so terribly. Angela was the South Dakota MDA Poster Child for two years: 1984 and 1985.

When you are in a tough spot, don't stop giving out to others. Jesus said that it is more blessed to give than receive (Acts 20:35). We receive physical and spiritual blessings when we pray for and give to others. As Angela served as the State Poster Child for MDA, for two years, we appeared on television on several different occasions. Sometimes the program official would just hand us the microphone and allow us to talk from our heart to the live television audience.

We expressed our thanks for the MDA support, and then we would encourage those watching to put their trust in Jesus Christ as their Savior and Healer. I used the opportunity to say, " We believe in a God who is doing miracles today, and some day, we believe that Angela shall be physically well again." Phones would start ringing and notes were handed to us of people that were encouraged. Many times near the end of those telethons, the song, "*You Are My Hero*," would be sung. We knew that the testimony of God in our lives was encouraging countless others to appreciate the blessings in their own lives.

At the television station, the MDA people would have a "hospitality" room set up so that patients, families, and special guests could visit. During one of the telethons, I found myself visiting with a young man with Duchenne muscular dystrophy. This is a terrible, debilitating disease. Most young men with this disease won't live past their twenties. As we were talking, he found out that Dave was a pastor. He became agitated and spoke with deep hurt that he hated God. Someone had told him that God had given him the disease and that this was God's plan for his life. How cruel for someone to say that to this man. Dave knelt by his chair and put his hand on his emaciated shoulder. Dave looked into his eyes and softly said, "God didn't do this to you. Someone told you a lie. Jesus loves you." At first, he resisted Dave's words. Dave told him again how much Jesus loved him. The words brought comfort and hope. He wept. Dave rubbed his shoulder and said that God still has a GOOD plan for his life.

We're so glad that God gives us Good News to share with others. The world doesn't need to hear your negative reports on what you think God cannot do. Just read Luke 4:18: "The Spirit of the Lord is on me, because He has anointed me to preach good news to the poor. He has sent me to proclaim freedom for the prisoners and recovery of sight for the blind, to release the oppressed, to proclaim the year of the Lord's favor." Jesus Himself was anointed to bring only Good News. He came to save, heal, and to deliver us.

Angela received letters from Jerry Lewis. Her story was written up in several newspapers. Sometimes when people would meet us in stores or at various events, they would break down in tears over our situation. They would ask, "How can you manage to go on in life?" We would always respond that it was the grace of God that sustains us one day at a time. We would feel His strength to encourage others and to tell them to put their own trust in Jesus Christ. Start serving lemonade. Talk about the blessings of God and not your problems.

Proverbs 13:12 says that, "Hope deferred makes the heart sick, but when the desire comes, it is a tree of life." Many times our hope was dashed by another setback. I began to hate words like "flare-up" or "relapse." But we must understand the full meaning to this verse. Hope is only deferred for a period of time. It's not deferred forever. He did say that the DESIRE, the answer, would come. Choose to focus on the fact that your answer is coming. In our situation, that took many years, but it is worth the wait! Hold on to Jesus Christ and His Words of hope. Combine patience with your faith. Do as Hebrews 6:12 says, "We do not want you to become lazy, but to imitate those who through faith and patience inherit what has been promised."

It is wonderful when we see the answers to our prayers come quickly. However, between the time that we pray, and the time that we see the manifestation of the answer to that prayer, is a time of faith. Don't give up if the answer does not come right away. There are many spiritual battles and we must do our part to keep our eyes fixed on Jesus Christ and His Word. Hope has power. We must not give up. You are not finished when you are defeated; you are finished when you quit. We faced many setbacks and the life of our

Angela's picture in 1985 as the South Dakota State Poster Child for the Muscular Dystrophy Association. Her face is puffy from the effects of the medications, but she never complained.

daughter was hanging in the balance, but we were not letting go of our hope in God.

Prayer:
Lord, You are my hope and my strength. I fix my eyes on You and not on my problems. I choose today to speak the positive things of Your Word. Thank you for the answers to prayer that You are bringing my way. In the powerful name of Jesus. Amen.

The Power of Praise
(Learning to Rejoice)

The Bible teaches us that God has provided a weapon for his people to use to keep us safe, to help us through dark times and to stay in victory. That weapon for God's people is found in the power of praise. Isaiah 22:3 tells us that God inhabits the praises of his people. He actually comes to live within our praises. During a long-term illness, it is extremely tempting to fall into discouragement and to allow a spirit of heaviness to come upon us. Another verse in Isaiah says that God will give us an exchange. He says He will give us a GARMENT of PRAISE in place of a spirit of depression. We are still the ones who need to do the praising. It is with our mouths open wide, singing praises to our God, that the atmosphere around us stays charged with light and life and miraculous energy.

We cannot tell you how many times one, or both of us, would begin to grow weary, but we would encourage each other, and ourselves, as we began to praise the Lord. We would start by faith to proclaim the power and the greatness of our God, the goodness of our God, and we would begin to thank Him for moving by His Spirit. We would thank Him again that He paid the price for our healing, and we would say out loud that it is with the stripes that Jesus Christ bore on his back that our daughter was healed!

In Psalm 81:10, the Word of the Lord instructs us to open wide our mouths, and God says to us that He will fill us! This is such a powerful discipline for believers, especially when we are in a time of faith, waiting for the manifestation of answers to our prayers. The Psalms are loaded with praise to the Lord. David faced many struggles in his life, but we see from what he wrote that he loved to give praise to God. We noticed without exception that when we began to praise the Lord, our circumstances may not have changed, but the atmosphere always did. We cherish the presence of the Lord and He tells us in his Word that in His presence is fullness of joy, and at His right hand are pleasures forever.

This reminds us again of the goodness of God and how He has only good days planned for each one of us. When we would begin to open our mouths, and give praise to the Lord, discouragement and doubt would lift. When we kept God's joyful presence, we also maintained His strength. We are reminded in the Psalms to "bless the Lord at all times and that His praise should continually be in our mouths."

In the Bible, even though David had been called and chosen by God to be the next king of Israel, he still faced much adversity. You can be in the perfect will of God but you still have an adversary, the devil, who wants to oppose you from being blessed. In 1 Samuel 22:1-2, it says that David had to run for his life from King Saul. He escaped to the cave of Adullam where four hundred other men joined him. These were not the most noble of characters. All of them were either in debt, in distress or faced great bitterness in life. Yet these four hundred men became the eventual leaders of Israel in David's administration. How were their misfortunes turned around? The answer to this lies in what David wrote in Psalm 34.

David understood the power of praise. God wants us to keep our eyes on Jesus and to focus on the promise and not the problem. Verse 1 says," I will bless the Lord at ALL TIMES; His praise shall CONTINUALLY BE IN MY MOUTH." We should let praise be a part of our everyday life and not just something that we might do at church. Verse 2 says, "My soul makes it's boast in the Lord; let the humble and afflicted hear and be glad." From this verse we understand that we can boast in the promises of God. David did this OUT LOUD in the cave and the other men heard him. In verse 3, David says, "O magnify the Lord with me and let us exalt His name together." We see that as the other men watched David, he encouraged them to do what he was doing: magnifying the Lord.

When you use a microscope in science class to magnify an object, you don't change the object. You just change your perception of the object. You see a much larger view of that object. When we magnify the Lord, we begin to see that He is much greater than our problem. Jesus is greater than sickness. Greater than financial debt. Greater than marital problems. Greater than the problems of life. Verse 4 says, "I sought for the Lord, and He heard me, and DELIVERED ME FROM ALL MY FEARS." David tells the four hundred men that as he prayed, the Lord delivered him out of ALL HIS FEARS, insecurities and doubts. This was obviously an encouragement to everyone who was looking at David in the cave. So verse 5 says, "They looked to him and were lightened, and their faces were not ashamed." This indicates that the men caught the revelation of how to be free from all that oppressed them. The praises of God set them free from their shame and their failures and from the attacks of the enemy. They became "worshipers" with David.

1 Peter 5:6 says, "Humble yourself under the mighty hand of God, that He may exalt you in due time." Just learn to do it God's way and to praise Him in all circumstances. Whenever you begin to feel overwhelmed, put on the garment of praise to push off the spirit of discouragement (Isaiah 61:3). The Apostle Paul understood this in Acts 16:25 when they lifted up their voices in a prison at the midnight hour and loudly sang the praises of God. You don't have to be ashamed of giving praise to Jesus Christ. Praise is your faith at work. He is your answer today.

Some Christians grow weary waiting for an answer to their prayer after two weeks. As a family, we had made a decision to LIVE IN THE ANSWER and to be people who would praise the Lord regardless of our circumstances. Even though it was not easy, this is a choice we made every day. PRAISE IS FAITH AT WORK. By choosing to give praise to God continually, we were already living in the answer, before faith had come to sight. We saw the answer to our prayers in the faith realm. We saw our daughter whole and well, and we spoke only words of life over her continually. Some days were easier than others, but most days were victorious.

Most people bemoan the time that they have to sit in a doctor's waiting room. We usually brought our Bibles so that we could fill our hearts with the promises of God. We also brought Gospel pamphlets, so that we could give them to the doctors, nurses, secretaries, medical aids, or any support staff. Let's keep making "lemonade" out of our situation. We got to know many medical staff on a first-name basis. They were friends to us. They cared about our needs. They knew about our family and as time went on, we knew a lot about theirs, too.

On one of those doctor's visits in 1987, when Angela's health was in grave condition, the Lord spoke to me as I opened my Amplified Bible to Habakkuk 3:17-19: "Although the fig tree does not blossom, and there be no fruit on the vines; though the product of the olive fail, and the fields yield no food; though the flock be cut off from the fold, and there be no cattle in the stalls; YET I WILL REJOICE IN THE LORD, I will exalt the victorious God of my salvation! The Lord God is my strength...and He will make me to walk and make spiritual progress upon my high places of suffering and trouble." These verses confirmed to us again to walk in the praises of God. KEEP REJOICING regardless of what you see with your natural eyes. God is working in the spiritual realm for your benefit and His Glory.

One day when we went to the doctor, he asked us how Angela was doing since the last appointment. We said, "Well, she's had more good days than bad." He laughed and said he thought that sounded better than most of the people he knew who weren't even sick! We refused to look at our circumstances, and for the most part, we did as the Bible says to do, fixing our eyes on Jesus and filling our mouths with praise to Jesus who is our answer and our healer. Worship and praise to God continued to fill our hearts and the atmosphere of our home. We proclaimed the Word of God regularly over our situation, over our daughter's body, over our son, Ryan, over our marriage, over our finances and over the church that we pastored. Every day and many times throughout the day and into the night, we gave praise and thanks to God for Jesus and for His healing power.

When our daughter was originally diagnosed with this disease, we searched the scriptures to find if there was anywhere in the Bible that God even hinted that He didn't want to heal her. Everywhere we looked, from Genesis to Revelation, we saw that our God is the same yesterday, today and forever. The book of Acts tells us that "Jesus went about doing good and HEALING ALL that were oppressed by the devil, for God was with Him." Then we read in Malachi 3:6 where God says, "I am God and I do not change." We were relieved to know once again that God doesn't change His mind. We knew then that no matter what we faced, we were standing on a firm foundation and that God would always stand behind His Word.

So many times, people base their beliefs on their circumstances. From the very beginning of this drama, we purposed that we would not be moved or shaken from the Word of God. Even though we could not understand events with our natural mind, we chose through the power of praise to rise to a new level and live in a supernatural plane. We rarely spoke of Angela's condition but chose to speak of her health, her abilities, her beauty, her destiny. Every day we gave thanks to Jesus for her healing. We tried to laugh often and created a faith atmosphere around our children by the words that were coming out of our mouth. Through the power of praise we were able to carry on fairly normal schedules. We did not allow negative words or attitudes to control us as individuals or as a family.

Our daughter was unable to participate in athletics. She was unable to go swimming or be out in the sun. She could not go ride her bicycle with the other children or ride horses or go down slides. In spite of this, she kept herself in an attitude of faith and developed other talents. She completed cross-stitch projects, puzzles, ceramics, and numerous crafts using her artistic ability to fill many summer days. Angela remained positive and full of praise thanking Jesus continually that He paid for her healing. As she wrote in her journal, almost always she would end with," I felt good today." We just didn't heard her complain or bemoan her situation. You could feel sorry for yourself, but what good will that do?

In the twelve years of standing in faith for our daughter's healing, we can only remember one time where Angela herself seemed disheartened and that was in 1989. At this time, she was around twelve years old and her elbows had become inflamed, swollen with sores and filled with calcium deposits. The doctors called it severe calcinosis. She had learned to live with pain and discomfort. They experimented with different medications like CoBenemid and Rynatan to see if they would help but they were not effective. The calcinosis was very painful and Angela could barely move her arms without extreme discomfort and burning pain. It was hard for her to even brush her own hair. One night after we had prayed with the children, they were lying in their beds still awake. We went into their rooms as always to give them another good night kiss and discovered Angela in her bed crying. There was such a heaviness in the room, such darkness.

Our little daughter had been fighting for so long and virtually never complained. That night, she was growing weary. As tears spilled onto her pillowcase, she softly whispered that she wanted to go home to be with Jesus. Never in all those years had Angela ever been so weakened or ready to give up. Immediately, we began to lift our voices again in praise to Jesus, that He had come to give us life, and He had come to give Angela an abundant life. We spoke God's word audibly (Psalm 118:17) that our daughter "shall not die but she shall live to declare the works of the Lord."

We raised our voices, boldly commanding the enemy of our faith to leave us, to get out of our home and get away from our daughter. Once again, a sweet peace and the presence of Jesus began to fill the room and though her physical situation didn't change immediately, the power of praise brought

Heaven into our daughter's bedroom. She fell asleep with renewed hope.

In 1989, the doctors recommended that we commit Angela to the Crippled Children's Hospital in Sioux Falls for long-term care. By this time, Angela was taking the methotrexate by IV in addition to the prednisone and plaquenil. They told us her arms would be severely bent permanently and that extreme physical therapy was needed due to the muscle atrophy in her body. Angela could walk slowly but she needed assistance to get out of a chair or to sit up in bed. She could not bend over or sit on the floor. Her arms were still too weak to hold any weight. When she was at school, someone was usually assigned to help carry her books and assist her with walking up stairs or opening doors.

We chose to keep our daughter at home (rather than the hospital) and to supervise her physical therapy ourselves. Each day as we stretched her muscles, we would pray scripture verses over her. It was a painful process. We were applying the principle of faith and patience. We would thank God for the "little victories." Any progress was something to get excited about. As the months passed, the swelling and pain left, and her arms and legs began to straighten beyond the doctor's expectations.

Psalm 149 says that when we begin to give praise to God, "it stills the avenger and silences the enemy." There is great power in praise. When we are yielded to the Holy Spirit and willing to let the high praises of God be in our mouth and a two-edged sword, which is the Word of God, in our hand; we actually have the ability to stop the enemy from his attacks. Jesus said He has given us "ALL POWER over all the power of the enemy and nothing shall by any means hurt us" (Luke 10:19).

The Bible says to resist the devil and he will flee (James 4:7). Over and over again, we would lift our voices to God and speak His Word, reminding Him of His everlasting Covenant with us. Reminding Him that He is a God who cannot lie. Reminding Him that He said to put Him in remembrance of His Word to us. He loves His Word and has forever established what He has spoken. We often found comfort in Numbers 23:19 that told us that God is "not a man that He should lie, He is not like man where He would change His mind, if He has spoken it, He will do it." His Word would not come up empty for us.

We place a strong emphasis in our teaching, preaching and ministry for people to audibly and unashamedly praise the Lord. He is the One who is worthy of all our praise, and the Bible tells us if we don't praise Him, the rocks will cry out and give Him praise. Praise is such a powerful weapon that is available to all believers. We must get past feelings of self-consciousness and self-centeredness. When we recognize what happens in the spirit realm, as we begin to lift our voices to God, and praise and thank Him for His goodness and for answering our prayers, we will continue to be set more free all the time. We should give praise to Whom praise is due. The just shall live by faith and we were encouraged over and over again to give Jesus praise for His finished work at Calvary. Just as God Himself spoke the very worlds into existence through His words, and by His Word the worlds were framed, we have the ability to frame our world with the Word of God.

What kind of 'frame' or 'picture' do you want to create in your world? It is up to us. Our world can be created by the words that come out of our mouths. "Oh, that men would praise the Lord for His goodness and for His wonderful acts among the children of men" (Psalm 107:8,15,21,31). Come on, let's praise the Lord together!

This is a picture of the Kaufman family taken by a newspaper in December 1985. Angela's story was printed several times in numerous newspapers.

Prayer:

I choose to worship you, Lord. You are my Savior and King. You are the One who gives me wisdom and strength. Thank you for what You are doing in my life and my body right now. I exalt you, O God and I will serve You with all of my heart. In the name of Jesus, I pray. Amen.

God Can Make a Way
(Trusting God for Your Finances)

When a crisis comes into our lives it can affect several other areas. With sickness and disease, there is the obvious physical realm, but there are also the effects on your family life, spiritual life, social life, employment and finances. In the case of long-term illness, the financial realm becomes a major issue. Even if you have health insurance, many items are not covered. Our situation was a setup for disaster.

We were in the midst of pioneering a new church ministry. The church initially provided our family with some health insurance, but we were trusting God for our very basic monthly needs and coming up short. We thought about what expenses we could eliminate and came up with cutting our health insurance. Everyone was healthy. We were young with no health issues. It seemed prudent at the time that insurance was an unnecessary expense. What are the odds that a young family would experience a catastrophic health need?

Two months after dropping the insurance, Angela came down with the initial symptoms of the disease. So as we began our doctor visits and then the intense battle to save her life that first summer, we also encountered the battle to pay medical bills. With each medical test that Angela endured, we asked ourselves the nagging question, "What will it cost?" Each doctor's visit, every procedure completed, and each prescription filled came with a cost. Of course, we were fighting the spiritual battle for her healing, but a huge financial battle also was now part of it. Thousands of dollars in medical bills to a family with few resources is daunting. The weight seemed overwhelming. Prior to this time, bankruptcy was a thought that had never entered my mind. Now it seemed a very real possibility. What do you do when the mountain you face seems insurmountable?

Jesus said that we should speak "to" the mountain (your problem). Your "mountain" needs to hear your voice! It doesn't help to talk "about" the problem or even to complain "about" the problem, but faith always attacks the problem. What does the Word of God say about my situation? In Mark 11: 23-24, Jesus says, "Have faith in God. I tell you the truth, if anyone says to this mountain, 'Go, throw yourself into the sea,' and does not doubt in his heart but believes that what he says will happen, it will be done for him. Therefore I tell you, WHAT-EVER you ask for in prayer, believe that you have received it, and it will be yours."

We realized that even in the financial realm, we needed the wisdom of God, and we needed to address this problem. You cannot ignore financial issues hoping that they will just go away. Don't allow bills in your mail to go unopened. Review every medical bill and check it for accuracy. YOU MUST FACE YOUR MOUNTAIN and speak the life of God to it. Scripture does say in Philippians 4:13 that "I can do everything through Christ who gives me strength." You can learn to have financial wisdom. You don't have to live in fear. Hiding from a problem will not make it go away. Paul goes on to say that "My God will meet all your needs according to his glorious riches in Christ Jesus" (Philippians 4:19).

The Bible says much about financial issues. Tithing (donating ten percent of your income to God) and stewardship are important attributes of the Christian faith. Some people view tithing as a practice that is outdated and no longer applicable to present-day faith. Nothing could be further from the truth. Consider that tithing was practiced before the law existed when Abraham gave tithes to Melchizedek in Genesis 14:20. Then of course during the law, the Lord spoke to Moses in Leviticus 27:30 that the TITHE IS HOLY. After the law, the New Testament refers again to tithing in Hebrews 7. In fact, if we can acknowledge that God is the owner of all that we have anyway, then a 10% tithe seems a small token to give to honor the Lord. Those who think that they own everything should remember 1 Timothy 6:7, "For we brought nothing into this world, and it is certain that we carry nothing out." Of all the funerals that I have participated in, I have never yet seen a U-haul following a hearse. You can't take it with you. But we can honor the Lord with our finances and live on His benefit plan. Proverbs 3:9-10 says, "HONOR THE LORD with your capital and sufficiency [from righteous labors] and with the first fruits of all your income, so shall your storage places be filled with plenty, and your vats shall be overflowing with new wine."

How will God supply? It is very important to set up a spending plan. Take a close look at every debt that you have and the income that you are presently receiving. Ask God for financial wisdom. If your outflow exceeds your income, then you must stop the financial bleeding. Don't continue to charge on a credit card for items that are unnecessary and unneeded. One of the fruits of the Spirit mentioned in Galatians 5:23 is "temperance" which means self-control, discipline or self-restraint. God gives you the power to have discipline over every area of your life, including your finances. You have the ability to restrain "you." We live in a world that has trained us to pamper ourselves. We love self gratification. We think that if others indulge themselves in various luxuries then we deserve them, too. At some point, we must decide to live within our own income and stop spending for what we cannot afford.

Facing large medical bills, we lived on a very lean budget. We seldom ate out. We never took an expensive vacation. We didn't have much money for Christmas gifts, but we gave a lot of love. As a husband and wife, we would communicate about every major purchase and usually even on the small ones. It is important to be in agreement with your spouse on financial issues. We learned to talk, pray and compromise so that we had unity in our decisions. Having peace in your home is a great buffer against all of the other stresses of life.

A couple of nonprofit organizations helped us with some medical expenses. We also qualified for medical assistance from a government program. In addition, we communicated on a monthly basis with doctors, clinics, labs and hospitals, that it was our intention to pay on each bill. Pay "something," even if it is a token amount. Let people know that you care and that you are doing your best. Many times we found favor with medical facilities, and they forgave a portion of the bill or discounted their prices for us. Be humble, be honest and communicate with your creditors, and watch what God can do.

In spite of our dire financial predicament, God began to show us His Word on finances. 3 John 2 indicates that He wants our soul and spirit man to prosper. God wants us to love and praise Him all the time. When we walk in His Spirit with this attitude, He also causes us to prosper in our health and finances. Isn't it amazing that God cares about every aspect of our lives: spiritual, physical and financial! Eventually, every one of our medical bills was completely paid off.

Of course, you will find some Christians who think that poverty is a blessing. When Jesus talked about the "poor in spirit," He was referring to being emptied of "self" and was not referring to financial poverty, as some Christians believe. Even our own government recognized poverty as an enemy and declared "war on poverty." It is time the church recognizes that Jesus came to destroy those things that hold people in bondage. Disease and poverty definitely fit into that category. He came to prosper you. He gave us a Great Commission in Matthew 28, and He will also finance it in abundance. Jesus was not against money; He just said don't put your trust in it. Even our government reminds us on the currency, "In God We Trust." God wants to provide for all of your needs. With God's blessing on our spending plan, I believe that we can have "more money than month." We can become "savers" more than spenders.

We can learn to trust the God who is called "Jehovah Jireh" and see the Lord's provision for every need that we have. You should read 2 Corinthians 9:6-8 in the Amplified Version of the Bible: "Remember this, that he who sows little will reap little, and he who sows generously so that blessings may come to someone, will also reap generously with blessings. Let each person give as they purpose in their own heart for God loves and takes pleasure in a cheerful and joyous giver. And God is able to make all grace and every earthly blessing come to you in abundance, so that you may always and under all circumstances and whatever the need be self-sufficient. So that you are possessing enough to require no aid or support and are FURNISHED IN ABUNDANCE for every good work and charitable donation." That sounds like prosperity to me! Just as we received a revelation that Jesus Christ is the Great Physician, it was also revealed to us that He is our Provider. He wants to meet every need that you have. Learn to trust Him today.

Most people have prayed the Lord's Prayer at some point in their lives. However, the power of this prayer can be diluted by repetition. Jesus said in Matthew 6:10, "Thy kingdom come. Thy will be done in earth as it is in Heaven." Think about this. In Heaven there is no sickness, disease or poverty. So on earth, it is God's will for sickness, disease and poverty to be eliminated. That's why Jesus went about doing good and healing all that were oppressed of the devil (Acts 10:38). Healing is God's will for today.

So why do we have sickness and tragedy in the world today? The reason is that we live in a fallen world that has been corrupted by sin. Romans 5:12 sheds some light on this. "Therefore as sin came into the world through one man and death came as a result of sin, so death spread to all men because all men have sinned." Accidents, tragedies and sicknesses can face all of us but the good news is that

Jesus Christ came to save us from our sins and to also set us free from these bondages of the world. "For this purpose was the Son of God manifested, that He might destroy and dissolve the works that the devil has done" (1 John 3:8 Amplified).

Therefore everywhere that Jesus went, He was in the perfect will of the Father to bring healing and deliverance to those around Him. In Luke 9:56, Jesus says, "For the Son of Man is not come to destroy men's lives, but to save them." The only thing that Jesus ever wanted to destroy was the "WORKS OF THE DEVIL," which are sin, sickness and poverty. It is never recorded in the New Testament that Jesus gave someone a sickness or disease. So when you are praying for healing, you are praying in the perfect will of God and according to the Lord's Prayer itself.

Think again. In Heaven there is no poverty or lack of any kind. When we lack the money to pay for our house, utilities, or to buy groceries, this is not the will of God. Now, certainly you have to be a good steward of your finances and not waste your resources frivolously. But the Bible promises us that God will supply all our needs. You want to believe God for His great provision for the things that you face. He loves to do things in abundance.

The Kaufman family is shown here at the Muscular Dystrophy Association Labor Day Telethon in 1986. KSFY-TV in Sioux Falls, South Dakota hosted the regional telethon. Dave had the opportunity, on several occasions, to tell about God's grace and healing power to a live television audience.

John 10:10 says that He wants to give you an ABUNDANT LIFE.

Be faithful with what you have right now. Use it wisely. Honor the Lord with your resources. Tithe to your church. Put some away in savings at the bank. Start living a life that is disciplined according to the Word of God. Most people didn't get into debt overnight and you usually don't come out of debt overnight. It is a long term process of paying off your bills. But in due time, you can climb out of those financial conditions and begin to live debt free. Jesus is on your side. Turn those financial burdens over to Him today.

Prayer:
Lord, I praise You today that You are my provider. I choose not to worry but to trust in You. Give me wisdom and discipline in my finances. I want to honor You with all that I have. Thank You for helping me with every financial decision I make. In the name of Jesus. Amen.

God is Good

When we want to get a good perspective of what God is like, we should look at Jesus Christ. Jesus said to Philip, "He that has seen Me has seen the Father" (John 14:9). The Bible goes on to say that Jesus was the "brightness of the glory of God and the express image of the Father" (Hebrews 1:3). Everything that we see and hear from Jesus is GOOD. He went about doing good. He blessed people. He healed people. He loved people. He showed mercy and grace to everyone. God is not harsh, judgmental, vindictive or mad at you. He loves you with an everlasting love.

During this physical trial, we were also pioneering a new church. We had attended college at South Dakota State University in Brookings and both of us had made commitments to Christ while we were in college. After we were married in 1975 in Sioux Falls, we worked in the business field for a few years. Then the Lord led us back to our college town to start this spiritual work. We were believing for our daughter's healing and at the same time, we were believing for God's blessing on a new church. These were two huge steps of faith going on simultaneously. When we started, we had no congregation, no money and no building. But we did have a WORD from the Lord. We had contacts with a couple of different denominations but we decided to become a nondenominational church. We rented meeting rooms for several years before we finally acquired some land and built a nice facility. Little by little, God added to the congregation and a vibrant church was established.

Now over twenty-five years later, we still pastor that same church, Holy Life Tabernacle in Brookings, South Dakota. What started in infant stages has grown to produce an abundance of good fruit. Thousands have been influenced for Christ. Several are serving on the mission fields in other countries. Some have received the call to pastor other churches. Numerous others are serving in church leadership positions around the country. Since 1996, we have also hosted many Pastors' Conferences that minister to hundreds of pastors from several states twice each year. God is good!

As we sought the Lord through all of our circumstances, it was so wonderful to see how good God really is. We would meet other people who would present this image that God is out to get you. Many people get stuck in the Old Testament and focus on the severity of God's hatred and judgment on sin. But we must remember that God sent His Son to abolish sin and to make a way for us to be free from sin's torment and to walk free in the Spirit. We now live under a new covenant of grace through the redeeming work of Jesus Christ.

We must see the nature of God through the pages of the New Testament. God sent Jesus to bless you (Acts 3:26) not to condemn you. Jesus defined His very nature when He said in John 10:10 (Amplified version), "I came that they may have and enjoy life, and have it in abundance to the full, till it overflows." When we understand how good God really is, we know that He did not cause our problems, but HE IS THE ANSWER to everything that we face in life. Jesus is on your side. He did not cause Angela's sickness. He did not cause your problems. Paul wrote in Romans 8:31 Amplified, "If God be for us, who can be against us? Who can be our foe, if God is on our side?"

Yes, we realized that God was on our side. This caused us to run to Jesus rather than run from Him. Jesus is your answer today. You can come boldly before the throne of grace. God is not here to judge you or beat you down. He wants to help you! Just read Hebrews 4:16. He wants to give you mercy. At His throne you will find GRACE to help you in your time of need.

Jesus prayed in John 17:15 (Amplified), "I do not ask that You will take them out of the world, but that You will keep and protect them from the evil one." God does not want to kill off His children. If He was killing His own people by sickness, car accidents or some other tragedy, He would be going against the very Words that Jesus prayed in the garden of Gethsemane. GOD IS GOOD! He is on your side. He desires to help us live victorious lives against the forces of darkness. He wants you to live a long life so that you will be a witness for Jesus and tell others of His amazing love. You are called to be an ambassador for Christ.

Our faith was far from perfect, and yet we always saw the faithfulness of the Lord when we turned to Him. Many times as I struggled to keep my eyes on Jesus and His healing promises, I would pray, "Lord I believe, help my unbelief." This doesn't sound so spiritual, but a parent cried out these same words to Jesus in Mark 9:24 when his son needed a miracle from the Lord. Jesus heard his cry and healed his son. Jesus would always meet us where we were at in our faith. Use all the faith that you have. Cry out to the Lord. Read and meditate on the promises of God for your situation. God is there for you. The Holy Spirit will help you. The Spirit of God will comfort you and give you courage to face your problems. He will guide you into the truth of the Word of God. He will teach you and give wisdom for the decisions that you will need to make.

Parents want to give good things and do good things for their children. God designed parents to act like He acts. He gave parents the hearts to have love and compassion for their own offspring. At Christmas or birthdays when children receive gifts from their parents, they are never worried that perhaps their mom or dad will give them something bad. They know the present will be something good, so they open the gift with great excitement and anticipation. A mom or dad loves to see their children receive a blessing. Parents feel good when their children are happy. God is blessed when we are blessed.

Matthew 7:9-11 sheds light on what I have been talking about. Imperfect earthly parents will always endeavor to do good things for their children, even if the children are naughty at times. "How much more will your Heavenly Father give GOOD THINGS to them that ask Him?" We praise God for forgiveness and grace. He is there for you. He hears your prayers. He is working even in ways that you cannot see right now.

In 1989, at a time when Angela was critically ill, I became desperate. Her condition was getting worse. She was undergoing chemotherapy treatments and the medicines did not seem to be helping. I was anxious and troubled in my heart. I went into a quiet place in our house and fell on the floor in tears. I didn't feel God's presence. I felt like I had been abandoned by God. I cried and complained before the Lord, "Where is the Lord in my time of need?"

As a father to his daughter, I wanted to have God give me her sickness. I said, "I've already lived a wonderful life and have experienced everything that I've wanted to do in life. I've been married to a wonderful wife. I've been given two awesome children. I have many great friends. I've had success in business. I've pioneered a healthy, growing church. Why don't you let me carry this disease for my daughter?" I cried some more. I laid on the floor like an old baby and finally I got quiet before the Lord.

God understood my heart, but then He spoke and I understood God's heart. He said, "Dave, as a father you want to take this disease for your daughter and that is exactly why I already took this disease at Calvary. I felt what you feel. I already paid the price for Angela's healing. I already carried every sickness and disease known to human kind." Praise God! I came off that floor with renewed faith in the One who gave His life for me and my family. God is good all the time! There are no shadows in God (James 1:17). He is not planning a bad day for you. In fact, His plans for you are for good and not for evil so that you can have hope for your future (Jeremiah 29:11). Jesus went about preaching the Gospel of the Kingdom and healing ALL manner of sickness and ALL manner of disease (Matthew 4:23). That's good news!

The wonderful thing about God is that He makes His will clear for an abundant life, and He gives us the power to walk in it. He didn't leave us here as defenseless orphans destined for defeat. He has given His children His power to walk in victory in our everyday lives. Luke 9:1 expands on this when Jesus gave the disciples the power to cure diseases and the authority to use the power. This is affirmed again in Luke 10:1, and He goes on to say in verse 19, "Behold, I give you power... over all the power of the enemy; and nothing shall by any means hurt you."

What are you doing with the power that God has given to you? It would seem foolish to sit in a car with the engine running, waiting for the car to move forward while the gear shift is in park. Many times we are waiting for God to move when He has already given you the authority to do the work. YOU HAVE THE AUTHORITY to move out in His power. Jesus told us to heal the sick (Matthew 10:8). "Freely you have received, so freely give it away." Jesus already said in Mark 16:18 that "Believers shall lay hands on the sick, and the sick shall recover." That's more good news! What are we waiting for? We prayed over our daughter every day for healing. We commanded disease to leave. It was wonderful to know that we were praying in the perfect will of God. Even as we prayed for financial provision, it was a blessing to know that He cared about our every need.

In 1990, Angela could feel a large lump in her abdomen. Our thoughts were attacked with the words of "tumor" and "cancer." Don't meditate on the "what if's" of life. The doctor wanted to operate but Angela's physical condition was compromised by the disease and all of the medications she was taking. We were always faced with the added "risks" of every procedure. After weighing our options, we decided that we needed to proceed with the surgery. Angela was in Sioux Valley Hospital for five days and the gynecologist removed an ovarian cyst the size of a grapefruit. During the surgery, the doctors did more muscle biopsies that determined the disease was still active in spite of the extensive drug therapy. We could feel Angela's hurt and pain, but she did not complain. Angela weighed just 85 pounds.

This seemed like another setback to fill our hearts with turmoil. In times of crisis, we must LET THE PEACE OF GOD RULE in our hearts (Colossians 3:15). Let your praises to God push out the fears and the doubts. Yes, everyone has his or her doubts at times, but you can have victory over those thoughts and let faith fill your heart. Sometimes there are many questions but few answers. Faith in God will give you stability in your thoughts. You don't have to be tossed on the waves of uncertainty. You will have peace in your heart as you think on those Bible promises and put your trust in the Lord (Isaiah 26:3).

Give your mind good things to meditate on (Philippians 4:8-9). Think about good health. Think about all the blessings of God that you already are experiencing. Fill your mind with good reports. The peace of God shall be with you. You don't have to understand everything. You just have to trust God and His Word that it is true. He is no respecter of persons. So He will do for you what He has done for millions of others. Knowing that God is good (all the time) makes you want to get up in the morning and look forward to a good productive, victorious and healthy day.

Prayer:
Lord, You are so good to me. Thank You for surrounding me with so many blessings. Thank You for the abundant life that You have provided for me. I receive this life and praise You for the wonderful plans that You have for me. In the name of Jesus. Amen.

Tragedy to Victory

When facing a long-term illness or some other tragedy, you sometimes wonder if there will ever be light at the end of the tunnel. After years of sickness in our home, it was difficult to imagine what a normal healthy family atmosphere was like. Yet, God would continue to challenge us to dare to dream about healthy days. Giving praise to God would help us to maintain a positive environment of faith. PRAISE IS FAITH AT WORK.

We would try to keep our faith current. In other words, rather than thinking that it will take God a long time to reverse the effects of illness, faith challenges us to believe for a miracle each day. Remember what 2 Corinthians 6:2 says, "I have heard you in a time accepted, and in the day of salvation I have helped you: behold NOW is the accepted time; behold, now is the day of salvation." The Bible is full of recorded miracles that happened suddenly.

It is important to be a thankful person. We chose to look at the things that we did have as opposed to what we lacked. Count your blessings. God wants us to live a lifestyle of THANKSGIVING. "In every-thing give thanks for this is the will of God in Christ Jesus concerning you" (1 Thessalonians 5:18). We understand the importance of knowing a "pass-word" when we want to gain access to a comput-er program. Psalm 100:4 says that we "enter His gates with thanksgiving and in to His courts with praise: be thankful unto Him and bless His name." THANKSGIVING is the "password" that brings us into the presence of God. Be thankful for all of the little blessings of life. Thank Him for the good health you do have. Thank Him that you can walk, talk, eat and sleep. Thank Him for your job and the skills that He has given to you. Complaining will never benefit your life. Thanksgiving will cushion your life like shock absorbers and help you to walk victori-ously each day.

In 1994, Dr. Drymalski told us about "IV gam-ma globulin," a relatively new treatment for auto-immune diseases. This would be an experimental treatment for Angela. With all of the various proce-dures done over the years, we would always have to weigh the risks. Angela was seventeen-years old, so we asked her if she felt good about it. She was will-ing to try one more treatment. She had a series of IV gamma globulin treatments done in the Midwest

Cancer Institute at McKennan Hospital in Sioux Falls. The ward usually had several cancer patients sitting in lounge chairs with bags of IV solutions hooked to their bodies. Angela was the youngest and the nurses were very kind and supportive.

The scripture says that His name is above every other name (Philippians 2:9-11). The name of Jesus is greater than the name of Dermatomyositis. It's greater than cancer. Greater than Alzheimer's disease. The name of Jesus Christ of Nazareth is far greater than that of any disease you can think of. There is power in that Name. There is victory in that Name. There is peace and hope in that Name. We love to speak the wonderful name of Jesus with reverence and love.

You don't have to understand healing or God's power. You just have to receive it. Most people don't know how their cell phone works but that doesn't stop them from using it. There are many things that we use every day, and we do not understand how they work. But we use them anyway without question or debate. You can be healed without understanding how healing happens. Receive your answers to prayer through faith in Jesus Christ. He is your Healer.

Angela was a good reader and an excellent student. She learned to play the piano, the flute and participated in the high school plays. Once she was going to a play practice and walked down some stairs. She was carrying a book bag on her back along with a sack containing a bag of potato chips. She slipped on the steps and fell on her back pulverizing the large bag of chips, but she was not hurt. It provided a good laugh for her friends.

It was difficult to play the flute when she had shortness of breath, but she persevered. There is nothing about long-term illness that is pleasant. Sickness is oppressive. Financial debt is a heavy burden to carry. After twelve years, we no longer could imagine what a "normal" life was like. Twelve years of doctor visits and countless blood tests. Twelve years of experimental treatments and hospital stays. Twelve years of regular travel to medical appointments. Being in places that you didn't want to be, but had to be there for help. Sitting in the cancer clinic for chemotherapy even though you didn't have cancer. Visiting with other patients that were worse off than you were. Seeing the tears in the doctors' eyes when you knew that they were doing their best but didn't have any other treatment to help you. None of these things are pleasant. But God is still greater!

When you are tempted to give up, don't quit! When you are discouraged and frustrated, keep praying! When you feel tired and oppressed, put on that garment of praise! When you feel lonely and that nobody cares, get up and go to church! The Bible says that we should follow them who through faith and patience inherit the promises (Hebrews 6:12). The two go together. Faith and patience are power twins. They work together. We must be willing and determined to hold on to the promises of God for as long as it takes. That could be one hour, one day, or twelve years. Never give up and never give in. Keep the faith and you can win.

You must just hold on with white-knuckle faith. When I was riding a roller coaster, I looked down at my hands holding the lap bar. I was holding on so tight that my knuckles were white. This is the way we need to grip the promises of God. If you are facing adversity, this is not the time to walk away from God. This is the time to run into His loving arms. Again, it says in Hebrews 10:35-36 Amplified, "Do not, therefore, fling away your confidence, for it carries a great and glorious compensation of reward. For you have need of steadfast patience and endurance, so that you may perform and fully accomplish the will of God, and thus receive and carry away (and enjoy to the full) what is promised."

Over the years, Angela had a team of medical specialists who worked on her case: pediatrician, rheumatologist, cardiologist, dermatologist, gynecologist, ophthalmologist, endocrinologist, physical therapist and dietician. One particular day in 1994, her head physician, Dr. Walter Drymalski at Central Plains Clinic, came to us and said, "You are the most amazing people that we have seen. You should be depressed, divorced, bankrupt and discouraged, but here you are still smiling." I acknowledged his statement by saying, "But you know the reason why we are this way?" He shook his head saying, "Yes, yes, I know that it's Jesus." Praise the Lord! We had one more Great Physician on Angela's medical team and His name is Jesus Christ.

Little by little, Angela began to get better when she was in high school and college. Inexplainably, her blood tests continued to show positive results. Slowly, her drug doses were reduced and then discontinued in 1996. Just as the sick recovered by Jesus's healing power in Mark's gospel, Angela began to recover. "Recovery" is not limited by time. It is a process over which the person continues to improve until the end result is complete. Angela's illness just took a little more time than some others.

She finished high school near the top of her class in 1995 and as salutatorian, she received scholarships to go to college. While in college, she met a wonderful Christian man, Joey Johnson, and married him when she was 21. We had only dreamed that she would live this long, and now she was getting married.

Some dads dread the cost of a wedding, but not me! For years, we had this spirit of death hanging over us, and now, we were having a CELEBRATION OF LIFE instead of a funeral. Hundreds of people attended the ceremony. Prior to Angela's wedding, she was accepted into the College of Pharmacy at South Dakota State University. She graduated with her bachelor's degree in 1999 and graduated with her doctorate degree in pharmacy in 2001.

Her health improved each year with no medication. Doctors monitored her case every year for a few more years. Twenty years after she initially became ill, her Rheumatologist declared that she was DISEASE FREE in 2003. He said, "You have scars, but the disease is gone." They don't understand how something with "no cure" is gone, but we understand that the Great Physician has been at work in her life and body. Glory to God!!

Currently, Angela and her family live in Sioux Falls, South Dakota. She works as a pharmacist for a major corporation. Her husband teaches business in a Sioux Falls high school. They have two wonderful, adopted children. They are servants for the Lord, and they are active in their church rejoicing in all that the Lord has done for them.

Over the years, I have often said in my sermons, "Why live on Grumble Alley when you can live on Victory Lane?" Currently, Angela and her family live in a beautiful house on a corner lot and one of the streets is named "Victory Lane!"

Our son, Ryan, is also married to a beautiful wife, Jennifer. Ryan helped Angela for so many years at home and at school. He diligently prayed for her healing with us. He sacrificed in so many ways for his sister, but God has blessed and promoted him for his humble service and kindness.

Psalm 40:1-4 sums up our testimony for Angela's healing.

Vs 1 "I waited patiently for the Lord; and He inclined unto me, and heard my cry.

Vs 2 He brought me up also out of a horrible pit, out of the miry clay, and set my feet upon a rock, and established my goings.

Vs 3 And He has put a new song in my mouth, even praise unto our God; many shall see it, and fear, and shall trust in the Lord.

Vs 4 Blessed is that man that makes the Lord his trust."

After many years of prayer, faith and trust, we have seen God deliver us out of a horrible pit. He has set our feet upon the SURE FOUNDATION of Jesus Christ and His Word. The Lord has put a new song in our mouths. People all over the world have heard the good news of this testimony. As a result, many have

Another happy moment! Angela graduated from South Dakota State University in Brookings in 2001 with her doctorate in pharmacy.

been encouraged in their own faith to believe for a similar miracle.

God is no respecter of persons. What He has done for our family He will do for you. Jesus loves you. He is your answer. He is your hope. He is with you right now. Keep your faith in Him. Good things are happening.

Prayer:

Lord Jesus, I'm not giving up. You are my Healer and my Provider. I am holding on to You and to Your Word with WHITE-KNUCKLE FAITH. Thank You, Jesus, for the answers and for all that You are doing in my life. I receive Your victory today. In Your mighty name, I pray. Amen.

Your Spiritual Destiny

Just call on Jesus!

Jesus said, "I am the door, if anyone enters by me, he will be saved." (John 10:9)

The Bible also says, "For whosoever shall call upon the name of the Lord shall be saved." (Romans 10:13)

Prayer of Salvation

"Dear Jesus, I believe in You. I believe You are the Son of God, that You died for my sins, and that You were buried and rose again as written in the Bible. I'm sorry for the things I've done that hurt You. Forgive me for all my sins. Come into my heart, take charge of my life and make me the way You want me to be. With Your ever-present help, I renounce all my sinful practices of the past. Cleanse my heart with Your precious blood. Write my name in Your Book of Life. I confess You now as my Lord and Savior. Fill me with Your Holy Spirit. Thank You, Jesus! In Jesus' Name, Amen."

If you prayed the Prayer of Salvation, we would love to hear from you! Please feel free to contact us.

CONGRATULATIONS on your decision to follow Jesus Christ!

Confessions of Overcoming Faith

* My body is a temple of the Holy Spirit.
  (1 Corinthians 6:19)

* I am redeemed (Ephesians 1:17), cleansed
  (1 John 1:7), and sanctified by the Blood
  of Jesus. (Hebrews 13:12)

* My members, the parts of my body, are in-
  struments of righteousness (Romans 6:13)
  yielded to God for His service and for His
  glory. The devil has no place in me, no
  power over me, no unsettled claims against
  me. All has been settled by the Blood of Jesus. (Romans 8:33-34)

* I overcome Satan by the Blood of the Lamb
  and by the word of my testimony. (Revelation 12:11)

* My body is for the Lord and the Lord is for my body. (1 Corinthians 6:13)

* I believe that Jesus Christ paid for my healing at the Cross of Calvary. I receive what Jesus has already done for me. Therefore, I am healed today in Jesus' name. My body is whole and my mind is well. (Matthew 8: 16-17, 1 Peter 2:24)

* My financial needs are met today in Jesus Christ. He is my provider. (Philippians 4:19)

* I am a child of the Most High God. I am a member of His family and I am a worshiper of His Son Jesus Christ. (Ephesians 2:18-22)

Things to Remember

* You are not alone in the crisis that you face. There are many other people who faced what you are facing. The Lord is with you even though you may not "feel" His presence.

* Remember that it is difficult for other people to totally understand what you are going through. Be patient if they don't seem as sensitive to your need as you think that they should.

* Try to maintain as normal a life as possible. Stay involved with your family. Don't pull out of the world. Attend church as much as it is physically possible for you to do.

* Don't be afraid to ask for prayer from others. The Bible says to call for the elders from your church to pray for you (James 5:14).

* Don't try to figure out God, just know that He is good. Keep your thoughts simple without analyzing everything. Be on guard to not blame God while you are waiting for your healing to manifest.

* Don't go on a hunt for sin in your life. The Holy Spirit will convict and reveal to you anything that is out of order. He is faithful to show us anything that isn't pleasing to Him.

* Rejoice in the small victories and physical changes for good, even if you aren't completely well yet. Be thankful that you are getting better all the time.

* As much as possible do fun things. Try not to take everything so seriously. Laugh several times a day.

* Enjoy God's presence and His faithfulness. Remind yourself that He wants you well even more than you want to be well. Be patient and relax until faith becomes a physical reality.

* Finally, be thankful. Take a moment every day to thank the Lord for all He has done for you. When you develop a thankful heart, you are changing your focus from how big your problems are to how big your God is!

Bible Verses For Healing

* Isaiah 53:4-5, "Surely He has borne our griefs (sicknesses, weaknesses, and distresses) and carried our sorrows and pains [of punishment], yet we [ignorantly] considered Him stricken, smitten, and afflicted by God [as if with leprosy]. But He was wounded for our transgressions, He was bruised for our guilt and iniquities; the chastisement [needful to obtain] peace and well-being for us was upon Him, and with the stripes [that wounded] Him we are healed and made whole."

* Matthew 8:16-17, "When evening came, they brought to Him many who were under the power of demons, and He drove out the spirits with a word and restored to health all who were sick. And thus He fulfilled what was spoken by the prophet Isaiah, He Himself took [in order to carry away] our weaknesses and infirmities and bore away our diseases."

* 1 Peter 2:24, "He Himself bore our sins in His body on the tree, so that we might die

to sins and live for righteousness; by His wounds you have been healed."

* Matthew 4:23-24, "Jesus went throughout Galilee, teaching in their synagogues, preaching the good news of the kingdom, and healing every disease and sickness among the people. News about him spread all over Syria, and people brought to Him all who were ill with various diseases, those suffering severe pain, the demon-possessed, those having seizures, and the paralyzed, and He healed them."

* Matthew 9:35, "And Jesus went about all the cities and villages, teaching in their synagogues and proclaiming the good news (the Gospel) of the kingdom and curing all kinds of disease and every weakness and infirmity."

* Matthew 10:1, "And Jesus summoned to Him His twelve disciples and gave them power and authority over unclean spirits, to drive them out, and to cure all kinds of disease and all kinds of weakness and infirmity."

* Acts 10:38, "How God anointed and con-
secrated Jesus of Nazareth with the Holy
Spirit and with strength and ability and
power; how He went about doing good and,
in particular, curing all who were harassed
and oppressed by [the power of] the devil,
for God was with Him."

* Mark 16:17-18, "And these attesting signs
will accompany those who believe: in My
name they will drive out demons; they will
speak in new languages; ... they will lay
their hands on the sick, and they will get
well."

* James 5:14-16, "Is anyone among you sick?
He should call in the church elders (the
spiritual leaders). And they should pray
over him, anointing him with oil in the
Lord's name. And the prayer [that is] of
faith will save him who is sick, and the
Lord will restore him; and if he has com-
mitted sins, he will be forgiven. Confess
to one another therefore your faults (your
slips, your false steps, your offenses, your
sins) and pray [also] for one another, that

you may be healed and restored [to a spiritual tone of mind and heart]."

* John 10:10, "The thief comes only in order to steal and kill and destroy. I came that they may have and enjoy life, and have it in abundance (to the full, till it overflows)."

* Psalm 103:1-4, "Bless (affectionately, gratefully praise) the Lord, O my soul; and all that is [deepest] within me, bless His holy name! Bless (affectionately, gratefully praise) the Lord, O my soul, and forget not [one of] all His benefits; Who forgives [every one of] all your iniquities, Who heals [each one of] all your diseases, Who redeems your life from the pit and corruption, Who beautifies, dignifies, and crowns you with loving-kindness and tender mercy."

* 2 Corinthians 1:20, "For all the promises of God in Christ are yes, and in Him we say, Amen, unto the glory of God by us."

* 2 Corinthians 2:14, "But thanks be to God, who in Christ always leads us in triumph."

A blessed family! Angela married Joey Johnson in August 1998. This picture was taken in November 2006. They have two adopted boys, Micah and Elijah.

About The Authors

Pastor Dave and Jeanne Kaufman have pastored Holy Life Tabernacle, an interdenominational charismatic church in Brookings, South Dakota, since 1981. Pastor Dave and Jeanne have walked through the valley of hardships and they have come out on victory's side. They have triumphed over tragedy. Their daughter, who was the State Poster Child for the Muscular Dystrophy Association, was miraculously healed and restored by the power of God after 12 years of sickness. God even delivered them from financial disaster as they applied the principles of the Word of God. They wear a garment of praise and exhibit the joy of the Lord bringing strength to people everywhere they go. They have a "Barnabus" ministry of encouragement that has brought the refreshing of the Holy Spirit to pastors and congregations around the world.

They have served in full-time ministry for over 27 years. Their faithfulness and integrity in ministry have been recognized by Governor Mike Rounds of South Dakota and President George W. Bush. Pastor Dave and Jeanne are living examples that show through faith and patience, you can inherit the promises of God. They have been married for over 31 years and have two grown children: Angela and Ryan.

This picture of Pastor Dave and Jeanne's family was taken at Dave's birthday celebration in early January 2007. It shows Dave and Jeanne with their son, Ryan, and his wife, Jennifer, along with Angela and her husband, Joey, and Micah and Elijah.

Contact Information

Pastor Dave and Jeanne Kaufman have ministered at numerous churches and conferences around the United States. Please contact them if you are interested in them coming to your area. When you write, please include any prayer requests or comments. Additional copies of this book are also available.

PASTOR DAVE & JEANNE KAUFMAN
PO BOX 654
BROOKINGS, SD 57006

Office Phone: 605-692-4616
Office Email: holylife@brookings.net
Home Email: djkaufman@mchsi.com
Website: www.holylifetabernacle.com